The Journey

*For Mom and Dad,
and for Grandma who believed*

Contents

The An of a gram

Compunction

Tragedies

Jealousies

Heartrending

Exhilarated

Obliteration

Uncertainties

Preservation

Dramatization

Manufactured

Interstellar Travel

Instant Messaging

The Tide

My Father's Tango

For Mabel Lee Hairston

The Jeweler

Triangle

The Tide

Richmond Farm Saturday Morning

A Love Poem?

The Jeweler II

White Dove

Pow Wow

The Appeal

Menu

The Life of a Mirror

Criminal

The Appeal

Bless You

Food for the Masses

Night Dance

Letter/Response

I miss Money

Notes

The An of a gram

Compunction

We are a shoddy unit—
throw in the towel. I can't take the count.
We can no longer travel in a punt
down the River Love. The moon
shines so brightly upon your tunic.
Still, I can't let you camp
on my land or mount
my hills. You must stay in motion.

Tragedies

I have to go on a diet—
I have sat in my life as if it were a seat.
You planted your seed.
It has blossomed and now it treads.
I want to die;
The thought of death fills me with greed.
Who wants to trade?

Jealousies

The air has been let out of the sail.
No longer do our souls
travel together. You have secrets you tell lies
and I love you less.
I'll jump in the sea—
my heart can't be in jail.
Your love seel
has been removed. I will sell
it to the highest bidder. We both lose.

Heartrending

You have begun to grate
on me. How could a love so rare
be eaten up by lies. Dishonesty has become your trend.
It has tried to consume me. The heat
rises and I must grind
this pain away. You cannot hinder
me from tending
to my heart. You cannot render
my love obsolete with your hate dart.

Exhilarated

Everyone, have you heard that hate
has left my life? I showed it the exit.
We made a deal
that it would stay in exile.
Before, I wouldn't dare
dial
anyone for a date.
But now I can't wait to hear
the voice on the other end. No rail
for safety. I hope it's not too late
for love. Does anyone know the going rate?

Obliteration

Today there is a bitter
smell in the air. Tomorrow I will nail
you to your lies. Nothing will alter
the plan. You can't bait
me with "I'm Sorry". It can't bail
you out this time. Did you toil
hard to attain
the liar's craft? I must obtain
sweeter air— I bolt.

Uncertainties

There are certain
comments I will not entertain.
You have used them to taint
this house. Others have begun to rent
a home here, where cancer
(rage) eats away the walls. I'm afraid to be so near
to homelessness. It has begun to rain.
What ties
in me are breaking? I thought we would canter
through our life; now it is a race.
Rage, when you speak please enunciate.

Preservation

I can no longer serve
you. That sweet verse
I can no longer sing. A vapor
called hate has begun to seep
into this heart. I will not praise
you, Aphrodite! You have caused tears.
Am I naive
to believe that time will cure the past?
Or must I spend the rest
of my life trying to save
myself from my reservations?

Dramatization

I can't maintain
my station. I've taken a train
to a faraway nation
and left you to raid
your heart. To ration
your love through the rain.

Manufactured

Nesha, Lately I have begun to fume.
We are not on the same team.
I can no longer follow your draft
of our story. The fact
is, maybe it was not meant
to be written. Love is not our best feature.
You've turn me into a beast. A calm nature
into a destroyer. You are not a compatible mate.
I don't know what else to say, damn!

Interstellar Travel

She times love's entry safely testing levels—
keeping the interstate
clear, waving off cars. Love is late,
there is no time to rest.
A letter
when read steals
her thoughts. Her volcano erupts, lava
explodes. The tint
of her face now red; a badge on the train.

Instant Messaging

You built a nest
by the computer. Waiting, aging
for that one message to be sent.
If it doesn't come what does that mean?
Has he made a tent
on some other girl's land?
He has failed the test!
The whole world is a mess.
The lovebuster gang
has struck. The teapot steams.

The Tide

My Father's Tango

The room was held still
in his Jack Daniels sway.
One whiff and I knew
the bottle had won.
Whatever he said in attack,
bounced off my skin instead.
An angry blue vein throbbed,
in his neck keeping the beat
as our tango began.
He pulled me towards
his hot alcohol-body and
I searched for something
to grab.
Outside sirens cry
for another crime
red and blue lights
jump from wall to wall.

For Mabel Lee Hairston

West Virginia 1936-2010 Long Island, New York

The garden is along the walkway.
Last year's white lilies, roses,
And those others
I have no idea the names of.
The lilies, sprouting
But not yet budded. The red rose stems
Barely out of the ground.
The others, which aren't flowers at all
But plants, fully grown
behind the plaque
In loving memory...

You loved your plants.
Some days I forget to water them.
Then night finds me in robe and slippers
Unspooling the green hose from the back,
Pulling, waking neighbors
Who surely think I'm crazy,
But you want your yard
The best on the block.

I'll make sure.

The Jeweler

I.

Angelic diamond that pleased the King of Kings so much that he made it flawless. I guarantee there is no diamond that is her equal. So pear-shaped, so radiant in every realm, I hold her above all. And yet I lost her in a field, she slipped through my fingers and fell to the grass. I lingered, heart-broken by my love for that impeccable diamond.

Since it slipped from me there, I have waited, watching for that sweet thing which use to rid me of sorrow to return. Oh how the mud has tainted her beauty, my perfect jewel.

I visited that field where she slipped from me in June, on the day the world was blessed with this jewel. On that ground where she fell grew roses, lilies, and daisies. My diamond was held captive there and I lamented at the thought.

A warm feeling filled my body and seized my heart. Although the words of Christ teach opulence, grief still took a hold of me. The sweet aroma entered my nose. The sweetness lured me to sleep and I fell upon the lovely plants beside my immaculate jewel.

II.

My body lay in the place where it fell, but my spirit floated and began a journey. This world was unknown to me, but I was placed among rolling green hills. No man could

(no stanza break)
believe the wonderful sights that captured my eyes.

The sight of the hills, fields and streams filled me with joy and banished my anguish and misery. I walked toward the stream, and with every step my body was filled with bliss.

When I reached the bank I felt the promised-land was over the water. I wanted to see the beautiful city, but the stream was too wide and to deep, yet I wanted more of this excellent feeling.

I wanted to know what was on the other side. I knew it had to be fascinating, for all that I had passed was lovely. I searched along the bank, looking for a way to cross. Then a familiar sight captured my eyes.

Beyond the bounds of the water sat a beautiful woman. She rose and walked toward me. She was familiar to me from her slender form and her salt and pepper hair. I knew her well.

Triangle

Four years on a plane has changed
to a triangle, and she is the vertex.
His station was her only point
but now she has two.
This shape that she created
is not equal but obtuse
with him at the farthest point.

The Tide

> "Like the sound of the tide uncovering
> and then covering the hard news of the day."
> Terrance Hayes, "The Whale"

It took me the whole drive home to realize
you would not be there waiting to ask "how was your day?"

It took me a whole eight hours to realize
I couldn't call you after work to tell you what happened.

It takes me a minute to realize
that when my phone rings it's not you calling.

It will probably take me a second to realize
that I no longer need to check on you.

It will probably take me years to realize
that all of this is not a dream.

It will probably take my entire life
to understand that you will never return.

The news returns each time it's washed away
and for loving you, heartache is the price I pay.

Richmond Farm, Saturday Morning

Great-uncle Hildred took me to the field
at six AM, telling me what they would look like
if they were ready. A healthy green,
green as a lily pad, he said.
I'd pick the unripe ones – it being too early
to pay attention, and anyway I was eight.

After the tobacco, we'd feed the pigs
in the pen behind the field who smelled
of musk and dirt and nasty water
and the scraps we'd thrown away
that was their food: apples, lettuce, old bread.
Slop.

Then Great-aunt Ennymo's ham and bacon and
scrambled eggs and toast and pancakes and
waffles. Were other people coming?
No, just us and my brother, Mom and Dad.
And lunch, just hours away, just as lavish.

After breakfast, Hildred had me hold the bucket
because I was too scared to milk
the cows that belonged to the bull
that didn't like me, although it was my job
to feed it. It charged the fence,
knowing I was afraid and waiting every Saturday
at this hour, giving me the sneer, the grunt,
the charge he never gave my uncle.

I hopped the fence.

                                        (stanza break)
Then a mile to the mailbox along the dirt road,
just grass alongside, a dog or rabbit running by.

A Love Poem?

> "How do you write a poem
> about someone so close
> to you that when you say ahh
> they say chooo."
> Nikki Giovanni, "How do you write a poem?"

What can I write
that isn't shown by my actions?
Will writing it down make
it real for you?
Why do I need to write
that a familiar scent brings my
heart and mind back to you?
With you I can be myself,
free from all of life's bullshit,
and sit down to dinner
and ask "how was work?
are you hungry?"
These are my love words.

The Jeweler II

III.

Her fine white tunic flowed as she walked. Her neck adorned with the loveliest of diamonds. The crown that encircled her head, made of the most vibrant flowers, huge diamond at the center.

Her face was exquisite with no fold or wrinkle. Her complexion was a pretty caramel. Her hair untied fell to her shoulders. I think if I had not seen it with my own eyes I would not believe any man's tongue.

When she reached the bank my mirth grew. She was so close and yet we could not embrace. That sweet entity spoke to me in such gracious tones. Delight took hold of my body as I answered.

Are you my diamond that I lamented every night? I have searched for you since I lost you in the grass. Hopelessness and pain filled my soul when I did not find you. Our parting has left me a dejected jeweler.

For so long I thought my diamond was misplaced, but now I have recovered you and I can rejoice. We can live in this lovely land, if only I could cross this stream, I would be an overjoyed jeweler.'

My diamond looked at me with sorrow. 'My ignorant jeweler, you have made two mistakes. First, you cannot live with me. Second, you cannot cross the river.

IV.

You say you would live with me here in paradise and cross this mighty river. But before you can cross, your body must be swallowed up by the earth.

How can you destroy my happiness and punish me with heartache once again? I have found the diamond that I had lost. What can be learned from continuing grief?

Why do you only speak of the bad? You must always praise God, for anger and mourning do not increase prosperity. You must endure his struggles and constantly seek his forgiveness through prayer. Maybe then he will take pity and oust your grief, but it is in his power to do so.

I did not mean to offend the Lord with my words; suffering has taken over my character. I pray for his forgiveness always. Still I long to dwell with you. This is a splendid place. May I see the city that my diamond has occupied for so long?

V.

You are not pure so you must view the city from the outside. Walk along the banks of the stream and find a hill. I ran towards the hill and rushed upon it.

Just as the apostle John had described the new Jerusalem *there was a wall so high that had twelve gates and twelve angels. Written on the gate were the names of the twelve tribes of the children of Israel. The city was pure gold and its foundations were garnished with all manner of precious stones. There was no light and no need for the sun.* My diamond walked away from the bank toward the city. She joined a procession of worshipers who were walking toward the lamb. I wanted to live in this place where happiness was abundant and everyone was equal. What joy it would be to remain here with my diamond.

I thought that I could swim to the other side; nothing would harm me for I had already suffered so much. But as my foot lightly touched the river, I was summoned back to my body.

I awakened in the field of bodies where I had lost my diamond. I was not displeased by my sudden return for it was not my time. But if what my diamond said is true, I will endure my sorrow and hide my grief. I will only take what I am given and want for no more.

I will cast out the bad and pray to the Prince for his mercy so that one day I can rejoin my diamond and be a serf of the Lord.

White Dove

There is a white dove
outside my window
and he sings to me every morning.
I hear his beautiful song,
like a songstress in mid scale.

Tell me white dove,
what is it you are trying to say?

My heart is so precious to me,
like the moon bidding the sun good morning.
It seems impossible that pain can penetrate it
or that sorrow will live there.
Like the white dove outside my window,
singing beautiful notes
in an everlasting range,

or like you and me happy forever,
creating notes with our bodies,
creating lyrics with our words,
but this song is no more.

I still long for you,
your eyes connecting with mine,
your hands around me.

White dove
with songs so sweet
that pierce my ears,
is flying towards me
like a lover toward his beloved:

(no stanza break)

Spreading his wings,
he shows no fear
of what could be or will be.

Come in white dove,
Share with me your perception of the heart.

Pow Wow

Grandma Thel from Westbury
has a surprise for us. Off we drive,
two cars' worth of family,
across Long Island and the 495
in a lecture's length of traffic.

We need to know, she said,
our heritage. She'd make sure.

Stiff-legged, I rolled out
onto the reservation, gated by
two green and yellow and red totems and a man
in blue uniform: *No contraband!*

What's 'contraband' – and is this jail? I joked,
and everyone but Grandma laughed.

In outdoor booths, someone was cooking rabbit
and talking about maize, someone sewed vests.
A man showed the way arrowheads were made,
banging a smooth silver rock to a point
with a larger rock wrapped in brown twine.
Nearby, someone aimed a bow and arrow at a photograph
of a black silhouette of a deer.

On a stage, there were dances for rain,
for crops, for food.

Grandma took me to the instrument booth
and brought me, the oldest granddaughter,
a black and red turtle shell

                                        (no stanza break)
with holes on the top of its back
and a larger hole that was its clay mouth.
She had one, she said, when she was small,
given her by her grandmother.

Her black hair took reddish brown in the sun.
Her light face, the tinge of red in her cheeks.
Her hands as she gave me the flute–
suddenly I noticed all those veins.

The Appeal

Menu

I pray to be released from captivity
so that I can live life off your menu.
You can no longer feast on my body.
My heart is a delicacy that you have grown to love.
You devour it daily in stew with a glass of red wine.
Will you ever choose another entree?

The Life of a Mirror

Sometimes I wish they could see what I want them to see;
But I reflect what's merely there.
If only I could show them. I'm the one in despair
But fingerprints block my view.
They only clean me to see their face.
How will it end?
Dropped, cracked, or split, never to be seen again.

Criminal

> "I became a criminal when I fell in love"
> Louise Gluck, "Sirens"

I prowl the night
following your scent. (Stalker)
I scoured your apartment
looking for clues. (Breaking and Entering)
I devoured the women I
saw you talking to. (Assault)
I place the cuffs on my wrists and lock them.
I race the squad car switching lanes,
its red lights spinning, its siren sounding
my arrival at my brick palace.

The Appeal

I.

Dear society of the United States,
thank you for letting me speak.
None of the other Negroes will vouch for me.
Let's just say my thoughts are controversial.
Do I still think there is inequality?
Picture the world squinting through a Negroes eyes.

II.

There are no longer cross burnings in your yard,
hate now hides behind
the interviewer. *Or* in the cop
who stops you for *prowling* his nice town.
Hate wears politically correct masks.
Martin knew he was hated,
shouldn't I?

III.

Living in this country, I think I've changed.
I've learned that: the cutthroat Negro
Will kill his own before he tries to kill the other,
the Uncle Tom Negro will agree with you
that racism exist only in one's mind,
the Hero Negro will always fight for
justice and equality for his people.
I ask; am I any one of them?

Bless You

Oh, I loathe the way you breathe.
How your nose whistles as it seizes air,
forcing it in.
I can picture that air
filling your lungs, battling to be free,
banging against your pink insides
until you exhale, hostage air freed
through a sea of bad breath.

Violator of air don't breathe!

Food for the Masses

Rocking tan *timbs*
with *Roc a Wear* jeans

spitting out rhymes
flowing through my head
contagious lines, I attack the masses
throwing the world into hip hop trances
through the fog

I prepare for the show

Relax my nerves,
'cause the crowd's on a high,
screaming for me, shouting out loud

I give them what they want
"Throw your hands in the air"

With my words they do what I say
pumping their fist to the sky

Gangstas bopping their head to the beat,
taking mental notes

Honies dropping their hips to the bass line
try to get elbow room to grind.

The Rulers back

Nike tattoo
"I Can" rule the crowd

                                              (no stanza break)
I am the answer to all the world's questions

The crowd is pushin me on
eating the knowledge
that I spit.

Night Dance

The moon smooches the sky,

licks the catalpa trees

and penetrates the leaves.

The plump leaves drip moonlight,

juicing the naked branches

that *lambada* the wind, caressed by the moon.

Letter

I wrote you this letter.
I'm sure you recognized the Chanel #5,
the curve of the F. But I couldn't
give it to you. My hand
trembles now at the thought.
So I place it on the table
with a paperweight to secure
its travel to you.

Response

I found your letter sitting
on my table protected by a paperweight.
I passed it a few times afraid
of what it would say. But
the longer I waited the louder
it screamed.
Finally, I rescued your letter
and sat in my comfy chair.

I recognized the scented pages
and the curve of your F.

Your letter with its
scented pages and curved F's
crumbled in my palm
as I flung it into the flames.

I miss Money

My Money has been acting funny
standing me up at dinner with friends.
embarrassed I do nothing
Just a smile and a head shake
"next time's on me".

I think my Money is cheating on me.
She gets so many calls from a Bill.
Who's Bill?
She never can spend time with me
off to pay Bill a visit I guess.
This Bill is getting all my Money.

I miss my Money.
We did fun things together:
movies, dinner, parties, vacations.
We had a blast.
But that's all in the past.
I've got a new girl now.
Her name is Broke.

Notes

"Compunction," "Tragedies," "Jealousies," "Heartrending," "Exhilarated," "Obliteration," Uncertainties," "Preservation," "Dramatization," "Manufactured," "Interstellar Travel", and "Instant Messaging" are based on word games in many newspapers. I used the following rules: end words must be anagrams of the title, four or more letters in length, and the anagrammed words cannot be changed to fit into the poem.

"My Father's Tango" is based on Theodore Roethke's "My Papa's Waltz" (*The Lost Son* and *Other* Poems, Doubleday 1948).

"The Jeweler" and the "Jeweler II" are based on the medieval poem "The Pearl".

The epigraph from "The Tide" as well as the line in italics are from Terrance Hayes' "The Whale" (Wind in a Box, Penguin Books 2006).

"A Love Poem" is based on Nikki Giovanni's "How do you Write a Poem?" (The Selected Poems of Nikki Giovanni, University Press of Mississippi 1996).

"White Dove" is based on Henri Cole's "Black Bear" (Blackbird and Wolf, Farrar, Straus and Giraux 2007).

"Criminal" is inspired by Louise Gluck's poem "Sirens" (Meadowlands, Harper Collins Publishers 1997).

"The Appeal" is inspired by Terrance Hayes' "The Blue Etheridge" (Wind in a Box, Penguin Books 2006)

"Food for the Masses" is inspired by Terrance Hayes' "emcee" (Hip Logic, Penguin Books, 2002).

In "Night Dance," the line "juicing the naked branches" is from Terrance Hayes' "Lighthead's Guide to the Galaxy (Wind in a Box, Penguin Books, 2006).